When Friendship Lives Beyond the Stars

A Resource Book to Help Children
Cope with the Death of a Pet

Written by Dr. Amy Sugar
Illustrated by Paul Miller

Published by Pawsitive Resources
PO Box 61 Midhurst, Ontario L0L 1X0
www.pawsitiveresources.com
e-mail: info@pawsitiveresources.com

Designed and Edited by Dr. Teresa Woolard
Designed and Illustrated by Paul Miller

Printed and bound in Canada

ISBN 0-9735704-0-7

Library of Congress Cataloguing

National Library of Canada Cataloguing in Publication

Sugar, Amy, 1970-
       When friendship lives beyond the stars :
       a resource book to help children cope with the death of a pet / written by Amy Sugar ;
       illustrated by Paul Miller.

Includes bibliographical references.
ISBN 0-9735704-0-7

       1. Loss (Psychology) in children. 2. Grief in children. 3. Bereavement in
children. 4. Pets--Death. 5. Pets--Death--Juvenile poetry. 6. Pets--Juvenile poetry.
I. Miller, Paul, 1946- II. Title.

BF723.D3S84 2004   155.9'37'083   C2004-903132-5

Preface

On January 27, 2003 I held my dog, Odie, in my arms as she peacefully left this earth. For 16 years she was one of the greatest joys of my life. She was the reason I wanted to become a veterinarian, to devote my life to helping these wonderful creatures that give us so much and ask us for so little.

After her death my devastation and sadness were overwhelming and stifling. My young daughter was very close to our dog, and now through my own grief, I also had to be strong for her. How could I explain this to her? How could I help her with her emotions as I was struggling with my own? My first instinct was to protect her from sadness and grief. I began researching and reading ways to help children cope with the death of a pet and I learned so much. I began with an explanation of death and answered her questions. I began to talk to her about remembering Odie in some way everyday so that all the good times they had and the friendship they shared could remain a part of her life. We reminisced about the funny stories, the tender moments each day.

One day, at the park she was on the swings and looked up to the sky – there was a large, fluffy white cloud above. She said with a huge smile, "Mommy, look it's angel Odie" I said, "You miss her a lot don't you?" She said "Yes, but look she's not that far away". That day really helped me – realizing that she was going to be all right. This allowed me to see some light in my own darkness of sadness and grief.

I was inspired to write this book to celebrate my dog Odie's life. She always had a special place in her heart for children and she would be happy to know that through her memory she continues to comfort children. I wanted to remind our children that the love of a pet, the precious friendship they shared is not lost; the friendship will always be present in their memories. My daughter now takes comfort in the belief that her dog will always be with her. She talks about her dog being up in the clouds at the park or sparkling from a star at night. I have found that supporting her through this emotional voyage has helped me with my own grief.

We all need to go through the difficult grieving process and to allow ourselves to experience the stages of grief (disbelief, anger, denial, guilt, depression and finally closure). It is necessary and normal but do not allow the sadness of your pet's death to be greater or longer lasting than the happiness your pet brought you during his or her life.

I recognize that the death of a beloved companion is extremely difficult for everyone in the family. I hope that in some small way this book provides help and comfort for the families whose lives have been touched by the love and loss of a pet.

Amy Sugar

Special Thanks

To the greatest husband, father and veterinarian, Dr. Darren Honest - for your love and support that provides me with guidance and direction down each path I choose in the journey of our life together. Also a special thank-you from Odie for all your excellent and gentle care over her lifetime, especially during her last few months.

To my wonderful Mom - for opening her heart to a little white dog and giving her so much love and care.

To my partner and friend, Dr. Teresa Woolard - for her inspiration, her vision, and her support throughout this project.

My sincere gratitude to Dr. Cindy Adams for taking the time to review this work and share her literary resources and knowledge on the bereavement process following pet loss. Through her dedication and expertise she is making an invaluable contribution to the entire veterinary profession. She is teaching our future veterinarians at the Ontario Veterinary College to be better practitioners as well as providing guidance for the volunteers at the Pet Loss Support Line at the University of Guelph.

What you will find in this book

A Note to Parents:

Suggestions on How to Use This Book

This book consists of two parts - a children's story and a parental resource guide.

Read through the parent's guide first to obtain a sense of what your child may understand about death and the emotions he/she may be feeling. This will also allow you to be prepared for questions and concerns that your child may express to you.

The children's book is a story about a girl's memories of her dog. As she remembers the good times she is also supported through her sadness and comforted by a friendship that is everlasting in her heart. As you read this story with your child, reminisce about your pet. Some of the pictures may remind your child of funny or special times with his/her pet. Remember that part of coping with grief is remembering the good times shared and learning to enjoy the precious memories. We need to remind our children that the love in their heart and the memories in their mind will allow their special friendship to live on forever. Allow this time with your child to be an open forum for expression of emotions from you both - from happiness to sadness and laughter to tears. Ensure your child feels comfortable that his/her emotions may be very different from other members of the family.

When Friendship Lives Beyond the Stars

This book is dedicated to my true friend and greatest inspiration –
my dog Odie.
Although she is gone from this earth, she lives on in my thoughts
and her memory still fills my heart with love everyday.

"Odie" (1987-2003)

When I was little I had a best friend
– we used to cuddle and play;

Now that I am bigger I have an angel to guide me every day.

Our friendship was the greatest; we had such fun

She always made me smile more than anyone.

Even though she is gone now, we are never truly apart;

She lives in my memories and in my heart.

Now she looks down from heaven to watch me play;

She helps me grow and learn,
keeps me company every day.

When it rains I feel drops like her wet nose on my face,

Her kisses on my cheeks, my hands – all over the place.

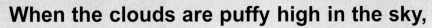

When the clouds are puffy high in the sky,

I imagine her fluffy coat and tail floating by.

When it is sunny outside
I remember her warm
body by my feet;

I felt happy, safe and cozy and she looked so sweet.

When I watch the
evening stars twinkle
in the sky,

She is there in my memories so I
never have to say goodbye.

Deep in my heart she is never far;

Our friendship lives forever beyond the stars.

At the end of each day when I close my eyes and snuggle in tight,

I say "I'll meet you again in my dreams my best friend – good night".

Special Memories of My Pet

_____

_____

_____

_____

_____

_____

_____

_____

_____

_____

_____

_____

_____

_____

_____

_____

_____

A Parent's Guide to Help Their Child(ren) Cope with the Death of a Family Pet
Talking to Young Children about Your Pet's Death

Of course you are the best judge of what is right for your child's welfare and well-being. However, here is some advice that may be helpful in getting through this difficult time. If your child is having an extremely difficult time coping, you may need to seek more extensive, personalized and professional assistance.

Death is a difficult subject for us to talk about. As parents, I think our first instincts are to try to protect our children from feeling sad or try to cheer them up when they do feel sad. We want to shelter them from hurt at all costs. When our children have experienced the loss of a pet, however, we need to allow them time to feel sad and support them through it. By saying or relaying to our child, "Don't feel bad or sad or hurt," we are giving a confusing message, not a comforting one. We are telling our children not to feel what they inevitably will feel. We will close the door to communication because they may feel they have to pretend or suppress their feelings to 'do what you have asked them to do'.

When discussing death with your child you will modify your discussion based on his/her age, maturity level and relationship with the deceased pet. It is natural to want to protect our children from this sad life event and shelter them from discussions surrounding the pet's death. We need to refrain from this as the child will ultimately feel left out and unworthy of our trust and this will be distressing to the child (especially to a child over the age of five). Discussion should be appropriate for young listeners. Be sure to avoid blaming anyone or discussing distressing details about the pet's physical state.

Young children tend to be different from us in their reaction to death; they are often more curious and open-minded. Try to be as honest as possible, use simple terminology, and speak slowly. Avoid using euphemisms such as, "Spot has gone to sleep" or "Spot has gone away", as these may lead to confusion and fear surrounding the child or others going to sleep or going away on a trip. Ensure that you explain to your child that death is not reversible. When explaining death you may want to ask your child what he/she understands about death and what questions he/she might have. Explain death simply – Spot has died which means he does not breathe, eat or play anymore; he is not sick or hurting. Of course, do not give morbid or frightening details. You may have your child think about how a flower or a tree dies (something he/she will have experienced). Try to convey that although death is sad, it is not bad or frightening. Stop your explanation frequently and ask if your child has any questions. Discussion should proceed based on the child's curiosity and extent of questions. Remind your child that he/she can talk to you about any concerns or emotions at any time.

Remember that, like with most everything else, children will emulate you and learn how to react from you so don't be afraid to express your emotions. Explain to your children that the emotions they are feeling may be very different from yours but the important part is to share their emotions with you. Allow your children to react in any way they feel when they are told about the pet's death even if their reaction seems inappropriate. Try to avoid 'cheering them up' immediately so that they are allowed some time to grieve and let them know it is all right to be mad or sad. Make sure they know that they are not responsible for the illness or death of the pet. Children often blame themselves for certain events even though there is no real basis for this. Tell them that nothing they said, thought or did made this happen. Perhaps remind them of all the great things they had done for the pet in the past. Children need to be encouraged to keep doing positive things such as planting flowers, making scrapbooks and other memorials for their pet. (See the section on Support Activities and Memorial Ideas, page 23). If an unfortunate mistake or accident caused by the child did have something to do with the pet's death, remember to discuss it with the child focusing on the fact that it was an accident. Perhaps recount a story of a mistake you made as a child. Most importantly, ensure your child knows what he/she did wrong and what to do differently next time. He/she will feel better having the knowledge and understanding to prevent this from happening ever again.

Another helpful tool is to have children recall their relationship with their pet from the beginning, for example, when they first met their new pet or even the planning stages of adopting the pet and then important events throughout the pet's life such as training and trips to the veterinarian. Encourage your child to recall the emotions he/she felt during each event and describe them to you. This will facilitate communication and expression of emotion when your child recounts the final days and the death of his/her beloved friend. Your child may not experience the stages of grief (shock, anger, denial, guilt, depression and resolution) in the same way as an adult. The stages may appear in a different order, simultaneously or some not experienced at all.

To the full extent possible try to be honest and open with your child about the death of your pet. Children will have negative feelings if they sense that you are lying to them. Do not fabricate stories about where the pet has gone such as saying the pet has "gone to a farm". Almost invariably children will 'not buy it' and it will be devastating to them when they find out the truth. Although the truth may seem more hurtful now, in the long run a lie (even with good intentions) will lead to mistrust and anger from the child when he/she grows up.

If your pet was euthanized remember to tell your child that the disease/illness or injury your pet had was the cause of the death and you only chose to end the suffering due to that ailment. Please remember that the death of a beloved pet is a unique and significant loss and should be treated as such. The loss of a pet should not been seen as 'practice' for dealing with 'more significant or real' human death in the future.

Commonly Asked Questions from Children

Some common questions that your child may ask and suggestions for responses are as follows (these will vary greatly based on your child's age and bond with his/her pet):

"Why did my pet have to die?"

Every living creature is born and dies – it is part of nature. You can imagine how a flower or plant dies. Most pets have a shorter time to live as compared to people. You may feel angry that your pet has died and that is understandable. In life we have many things happen, some make us happy (remember when you used to play with 'Fluffy' how that made you so happy) and some make us sad (like the loss of your pet).

"Why couldn't the vet save my pet?"

Veterinarians can do many things to help sick or injured animals but sometimes an animal cannot be saved. Veterinarians and staff at the animal hospital love all animals and try to do everything possible to keep a pet healthy so that he/she can enjoy life. (You can enlist your veterinarian's help explaining the illness or injury to your child – especially an older child who may have questions for the veterinarian.)

"Is death like sleeping?"

No, death is nothing like sleeping. Everyone needs sleep to rest while they are alive. Living creatures will wake up after a rest. Once an animal dies he/she will not come back to life. When a pet dies his/her body does not work anymore – the pet does not need to eat or sleep or breathe anymore.

"Why did my friend say I was silly to be sad because Fluffy was 'just an animal'?"

Sometimes people say things like that because they don't understand. Maybe your friend has never had the great friendship and love of a pet like you had with your pet. No one should ever tell you what you can or cannot feel. For now, maybe find someone else to talk to about how you are feeling that does understand. You have every right to feel sad or lonely or mad and you have every right to cry if you feel like it.

"When will I stop feeling sad?"

Everyone is different in how long it takes him/her to grieve. Take all the time you need to feel sad over your loss. With time you will be able to think about all the happy moments you shared with your pet and remember that in your heart your special friendship can live forever.

Children's Perceptions of Death and Age – Specific Advice

Infants to 1 year of age: They do not have a true understanding of death.

★ Even though the infant will not understand the situation he/she may sense tension and sadness in the family.
★ When possible try to remove the infant from an extremely distressing environment.
★ Try to get child care help from friends and family to allow yourself a chance to grieve and allow your emotions to be expressed.
★ Lots of extra affection will likely help both of you during this time.

Children 2-4 years of age: They do not have a clear understanding of death or of what they are feeling emotionally. They will not recognize the permanence of death.

★ Give lots of reassurance through hugs and help explain the situation using tools such as books or storytelling.
★ Recognize that the emotions they are feeling may be new to them and they will look to you for how to react to these emotions.
★ Encourage the child to express his/her emotions through play e.g. pictures, pretend funeral services, play with toy animals.
★ The child may 'act out' with undesirable behavior such as tantrums or sleep disturbances. Try to be patient and understand what specifically is bothering the child.
★ Explain death simply and honestly – use phrases such as your pet is dead which means he/she will not eat or breathe or move again. Expand upon this based on the child's questions.
★ Reassure the child that he/she is in no way responsible for the illness or death in anything he/she did or thought as young children often blame themselves.
★ Do not use terms like pet was 'put to sleep' or pet 'has gone far away' as this may invoke fears of going to sleep or others 'going away' as on a vacation.
★ Do not say that others who have died wanted the pet for companionship in heaven as the child may become angry with the deceased person or fearful that he/she will be taken too.
★ Allow time for your child to be sad and mourn in his/her own way.

★ Your child may surprise you by reacting with very little emotion. This is normal due to the problems children have with understanding the permanence of death at this age.

Children 5-10 years of age: They do have an understanding about death but are unclear about what causes death or that it happens to all living creatures. They often feel it can be avoided. Usually, around 9-10 years of age, children begin to understand that death is not reversible and comes to all living things.

★ Involve your child in as many decisions as possible regarding the aftercare and memorials for the pet.
★ Give your child lots of opportunity to express his/her emotions and ask questions about death.
★ Encourage your child to plan memorials for the pet as this is especially important for this age group. (See the section on Support Activities and Memorial Ideas, page 23).
★ Be especially sensitive that certain times of the day may be more difficult if he/she shared special activities with the pet at that time (e.g. walking the dog after school or feeding the cat before breakfast).

Children 11-16 years of age: They understand the permanence of death and may feel a sense of powerlessness. They feel the pet was their own yet they may perceive that the 'decision making' surrounding the death is being taken over by their parents – this will be very distressing to this age group.

★ Allow your teenager to participate in as many decisions about the aftercare and memorials for the pet as possible.
★ Try to avoid arguing with your teenager about his/her views of the pet's death. Be supportive without criticizing and perhaps offer to discuss his/her opinions at a later, less emotionally charged, time.
★ Enlist the help of your veterinarian if your teenager has outstanding medical questions surrounding the pet's illness (or accident) and death.
★ Older teenagers may grieve in a way very similar to adults.

In summary, as you are supporting your children through the loss of their pet, remember the following:

P lan activities with your children to work through their grief and emotions.

E xpress your emotions to your children so they know it is all right to feel sad and that your sadness is not related to anything they did.

T alk to your children about death and grieving.

L isten to your children's questions and concerns.

O pen your mind to understand how they may think or feel.

S implify your discussion so they understand and feel included.

S ensitively deal with behavior or sleep disruptions during this difficult time.

While caring for and supporting your child through the grieving process you may feel you need some support and help as well. *The Loss of a Pet* by Wallace Sife, PhD is an excellent book. *When Children Grieve* by John W. James and Russell Friedman (with Dr. Leslie Landon Matthews) is another excellent resource that guides you in helping your child through many different losses in life. There are numerous pet loss support groups/hotlines throughout North America. Check with your veterinarian or a veterinary teaching hospital closest to you for detailed information.

Support Activities and Memorial Ideas

★ Plant a tree in your backyard – you may even want to choose one as a family that 'reminds' you of the pet. For example, a snowball bush for a white, fluffy dog/cat or a big, oak tree for a working breed dog.

★ Plant flowers yearly in a flower bed and take that time to reminisce and remember the pet. Each family member can pick their own flower and prepare one story about the pet to share with the others.

★ Have all family members wear something that reminds them of the pet. For example, get all shirts to match the same color as the pet's favorite collar, get a picture of your pet on a nightshirt, a ring with the pet's birthstone or engrave the pet's name in a locket.

★ Make each family member a small pillow out of the pet's favorite blanket or bandana.

★ Celebrate the pet's birthday with a cake and reminisce about all the good times.

★ Hold a memorial service – let your child take part in the planning as much as possible (older children can do the planning/inviting independently).

★ Start a scrapbook with photos, drawings and/or stories.

★ Make a donation in the pet's name and let your child choose the charity.

★ Write a letter or a 'will' from the pet – this will serve as a nice family activity to share and a forum for memories and stories.

★ Have all family members write (or if they are too young, you can do it for them) a letter to the pet to express their feelings or perhaps things they wish they could say to the pet.

★ Keep a list (all family/friends can add to this) of all the things your pet did that made you smile or laugh. Your family can experience the joy your pet brought to their lives now and for years to come.

★ Help your children write out memories of their entire relationship with their pet. You can use the page entitled, "Special Memories of My Pet" in this book on page 18. You can start with their first memories of meeting their pet (if they were old enough to remember) to significant events they shared together. Some examples include: getting permission to have a pet, naming the pet, housebreaking and training, trips to the veterinarian, getting sick, emotions about the final day with the pet. Discussion of these events can help to create an environment where your children feel comfortable expressing their emotions and you can support them through this.

A Difficult Question – When Should We Get Another Pet?

There is no easy answer to this question and really no right or wrong. It is an individual decision based on many factors. Although you will likely receive a lot of advice about when or if you should welcome a new pet, never let anyone talk you into getting one before you feel your family is ready.

Remember that your child needs some time to feel sad because he/she has suffered a devastating loss. Above all else, do not try to rush in and 'fix' everything with a new pet. The bond between children and their pets is as unique as each of their personalities so it can never be replaced. Thus, allow yourselves and your children a grief period. In some cases if you acquire a new pet too quickly your child (especially over the age of 5) may not have had a chance to grieve and reach closure. As much as we always want to protect our children from hurt and sadness, do allow your children to grieve or they may have unresolved emotional issues later. If your toddler is reacting with behavior or sleep problems, you may consider getting a new pet sooner if you feel this may help him/her.

Make sure you explain to your child (gauge this to his/her level of understanding, of course) that a new pet may be very different from the other pet and is never meant to replace the pet that has died. Tell your child that each animal is unique, just as every person is unique, and we should appreciate the differences as well as the similarities. We need to convey that neither the pet nor the relationship with the pet can ever be replaced. With this in mind, some experts caution against getting a new pet of the same breed/type and sex. Practically though, some families choose a certain breed for personality type or care requirements since this fits with their lifestyle. Under these circumstances I wouldn't hesitate to get the same breed/type of pet as long as your child understands that this pet is a new personality and that means a new relationship. I would, however, avoid giving the same name such as "Teddy Too" (if the deceased pet was named Teddy) as this will send confusing messages to your child.

Remind your child how loving and caring he/she was to the other pet and explain that a new pet would benefit from his/her friendship and love. Take cues from your child. You are the best judge of whether everyone is emotionally ready to welcome a new pet. Discuss your feelings as a family and allow everyone to have a say in whether they are ready to accept a new pet. When everyone is ready, involve your child (or children) as much as possible in the selection process and preparations for the new pet.

Resources Used for this Book

1) Adams, Cindy, MSW, PhD. Assistant Professor, Ontario Veterinary College, University of Guelph, Guelph, Ontario, Canada

2) Adams, Cindy, Dr. and Cohen, Susan Dr. *Pet Loss and Client Grief.* Continuing Education CD-Rom. Guelph, Ontario, Lifelearn Inc., 1999

3) Carmack, Betty J. *The Effects on Family Members and Functioning After the Death of a Pet.* Pets and The Family. Haworth Press, 1985

4) Colorado State University Veterinary Teaching Hospital. *Children's Grief Packet.* Colorado

5) Garcia, Eddie DVM. *Pet Loss Considered from the Veterinary Perspective.* Norden News, 1986

6) James, John W. and Friedman, Russell with Matthews, Dr. Leslie Landon. *When Children Grieve.* New York, HarperCollins, 2001

7) Mahon, Eugene MD and Simpson, Dawn MA, RN. *The Painted Guinea Pig.* (year and publisher unknown)

8) Rosenberg, Marc A. VMD. *Clinical Aspects of the Grief Associated With the Loss of a Companion Pet.* Canine Practice, May-June, Vol 8, No.3, 1981

9) Sife, Wallace PhD. *The Loss of A Pet.* Canada, John Wiley and Sons, 1998

To Contact us

★ We would appreciate hearing how this book has helped your family during this difficult time. If you are interested in ordering additional copies for either yourself or for friends and family, please contact us at:

Pawsitive Resources	
P.O. Box 61, Midhurst, ON L0L1X0	www.pawsitiveresources.com
Fax:(705) 733-9178	info@pawsitiveresources.com